Take a trip to
INDIA

Keith Lye

General Editor
Henry Pluckrose

Franklin Watts
London   New York   Sydney   Toronto

Words about India

Agra

bicycle
  rickshaws
Buddhism

Calcutta
chapattis
chillis
classical dances
curries

Darjeeling
Delhi
dialects

embroidery

farm machinery

Ganges

Himalayas
Hindi
Hinduism

Islamic
  Republic

Jagannatha
Jainism

Kali
Krishna

logging

mahouts
Moslems

nursery beds

paddies
paise
Parliament
pilgrims

republic
rupee

sari
Sikhism

Taj Mahal
threshing

Varanasi

Franklin Watts Limited
8 Cork Street
London W1

ISBN UK edition: 0 85166 984 0
ISBN US edition: 0 531 04347 9
Library of Congress Catalog Card No:
82–50306

Typeset by Ace Filmsetting Ltd.,
Frome, Somerset
Printed in Great Britain by
E. T. Heron, Essex and London

Maps: Tony Payne
Design and Editorial Services:
Grub Street
Photographs: Zefa; J. J. Andrew, 4,
18, 20, 22, 27, front cover, back
cover; G. Burns, 28; D. Turner, 8.

India is the world's seventh largest country. It has a population of nearly 700 million. Only China has more people. To the north of India lie the Himalayan mountains. The snow in the mountains feeds many of India's rivers.

The Ganges is India's largest river. It rises in the icy Himalayas and flows across the warm plains of northern India. Farmers use the Ganges to grow crops. These plains have fertile soils and are heavily populated.

4

This picture is a bird's eye view of the Thar desert. This large desert is in north-west India, near the border with Pakistan. Few people live in this dry, sandy region. Camels are the main means of transport.

New Delhi, the capital of India, was built in 1912 near Old Delhi. India's Parliament Building is in New Delhi. India is now a republic. The subcontinent of India was ruled by Britain from the 18th century until 1947. It was then split into two independent nations: India and Pakistan.

India is one of the world's poorest countries. Many people try to find work in cities. Calcutta, India's largest city, has 7 million people. Many cities have too few houses and people live in slums.

This picture shows some of the stamps and money used in India. The main unit of currency is the rupee, which is divided into 100 paise.

8

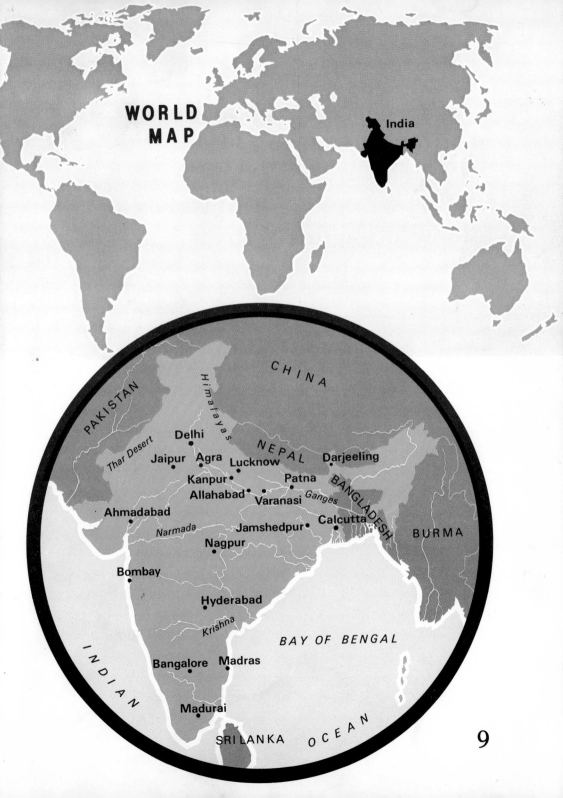

WORLD MAP

India

CHINA

PAKISTAN

Himalayas

Thar Desert

Delhi

Jaipur Agra Lucknow

NEPAL

Darjeeling

Kanpur

Patna

BANGLADESH

Allahabad Varanasi

Ganges

Ahmadabad

Narmada

Jamshedpur Calcutta

BURMA

Nagpur

Bombay

Hyderabad

Krishna

BAY OF BENGAL

INDIAN

Bangalore Madras

Madurai

SRI LANKA OCEAN

9

Bombay is India's second largest city, with nearly 6 million people. It is a commercial and industrial city, with tall office buildings. Bombay is India's chief seaport. It stands on an island facing the Arabian Sea. Its university was founded in 1857.

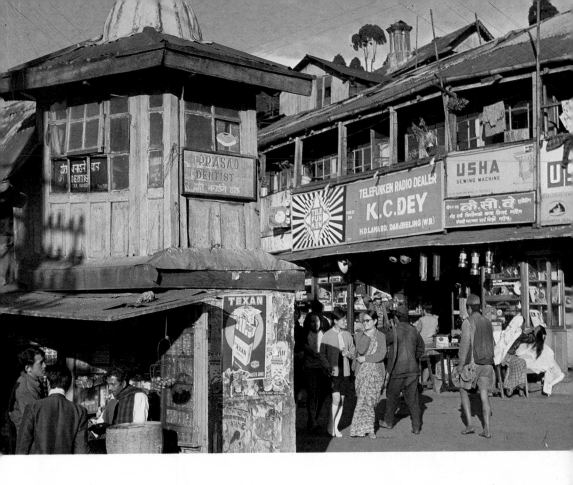

Darjeeling, a town in north-east India, stands in the foothills of the Himalayas. It has cool summers, unlike the plains to the south. Darjeeling lies in the middle of a tea-planting area. In the town, there are many stores open to the street.

India leads the world in producing
a number of crops, including tea. Tea
is grown in warm, rainy areas on
large plantations. Workers collect tea-
leaves in baskets which they carry on
their backs. The leaves then go to a
factory where the tea is cured.

Rice is India's leading food crop. Only China grows more rice than India. Young plants are often grown from seed in nursery beds. The seedlings are then removed and transplanted in flooded fields called paddies. Rice grows well in wet soil.

The Bhakra and Nangal dams lie
north of Delhi in north-west India.
These dams provide hydro-electric
power and water for large areas.
Indian farmers use this water to
turn wasteland into farmland.

This steel mill is in Calcutta, which stands on the Hooghly River, a branch of the Ganges, not far from the Bay of Bengal. Industry employs only one out of every ten people. But mining and manufacturing are becoming more important.

Indian children attend free primary schools for four to five years. But many areas have no schools and many children leave school at an early age. As a result, 64 out of every 100 Indians cannot read or write.

These girls live in the north-western state of Himachal Pradesh. They work on a tea plantation. About 75 out of every 100 people in India work on the land.

Indian women wear beautiful dresses called saris. A sari is a long piece of cloth which a woman winds around herself, with the loose end over her head or her shoulders. India is also famous for its embroidery.

18

Many people in Old Delhi travel around on bicycles. Sometimes a whole family is seen on a single bicycle. In this picture there are many bicycle rickshaws which travel quickly through the narrow, crowded streets. Only the rich own cars.

These people are threshing grain. Many farmers in India produce only enough food to feed their families. They have no money for modern machinery and do most of the work by hand. If the rains do not come, food is scarce, and the people may starve.

Indian elephants are taught to do work by men called mahouts. Elephants are important in logging, because they can shift heavy logs in places where machines cannot go. They also transport cargo and people.

Food stalls are common in the cities. Many Indians do not eat meat, but they like spicy foods called curries. Some curries contain chillies and are hot. Flat pancakes made from flour are called chapattis. They are eaten instead of bread or rice.

This is a temple to the Hindu goddess Kali in Calcutta. Today, out of every 100 people in India, 83 are Hindus and 11 are Moslems. Other major religions include Christianity, Sikhism, Buddhism and Jainism.

This is the temple of Jagannatha, one of the forms of the Hindu god Krishna. There are many stories about Krishna's adventures. The temple is in Udaipur, in western India.

This Moslem mosque is in Delhi. When British India was divided in 1947 into two nations, many Moslems went to Pakistan, which became an Islamic Republic. But many others stayed in India where they are free to worship in their own way.

No one will harm this cow in Varanasi. Although cattle are used as beasts of burden, cows are sacred to Hindus. Varanasi is on the River Ganges in north-central India.

Varanasi is a holy city. Hindus go there to bathe in the River Ganges. They believe that the waters of this sacred river will wash away all their sins. Hindu pilgrims also visit the temples in Varanasi and make offerings to their gods.

Many people in India travel by rail. India is a big country with the world's fourth largest rail network. Some 15 main languages and hundreds of dialects are spoken in India. India has two official languages. They are Hindi and English.

This is an open-air book stall in
Bombay. Educational books are
prized in India. Indians believe that
education is very important, because
only educated people can raise the
country's standard of life.

These dancers in north-west India wear strange masks and costumes. Each movement they make has a meaning. Indian culture dates back at least 4,500 years. Many great civilizations existed in India long before it was part of the British Empire.

The Taj Mahal is in Agra, south of Delhi. It was built between 1632 and 1653 by the ruler Shah Jehan. It was a memorial to his wife. The bodies of Shah Jehan and his wife lie beneath a central room in the building.

Index

EDGE
BOOKS™

◉•◦•⟫— THE GREAT OUTDOORS —⟪•◦•◉

ICE FISHING

Revised and Updated

by Laura Purdie Salas

Consultants:

Kathy Beaulieu
MinnAqua Education Program
Minnesota Department
of Natural Resources

Scott Gustafson
Fisheries Specialist
Minnesota Department
of Natural Resources

Capstone
press®

Mankato, Minnesota

Edge Books are published by Capstone Press,
151 Good Counsel Drive, P.O. Box 669, Mankato, Minnesota 56002.
www.capstonepress.com

Library of Congress Cataloging-in-Publication Data
Salas, Laura Purdie.
Ice fishing / by Laura Purdie Salas.—Rev. and updated.
p. cm.—(The great outdoors)
Includes bibliographical references and index.
ISBN-13: 978-1-4296-0822-0 (hardcover)
ISBN-10: 1-4296-0822-6 (hardcover)
1. Ice fishing—Juvenile literature. I. Title. II. Series.
SH455.45.S23 2008
799.12'2—dc22   2007007724

Summary: Describes the history, equipment, techniques, conservation issues, rules, and safety concerns related to the sport of ice fishing.

Editorial Credits
Carrie Braulick, editor; Tom Adamson, revised edition editor; Thomas Emery, revised edition designer; Kyle Grenz, revised edition production designer

Photo Credits
Tom Stack and Associates, 10
Capstone Press Studio, all other images

Capstone Press thanks Jamie Fessel for the use of his ice house for photo shoots, and Cabela's in Owatonna, Minnesota, for additional help with photo shoots.

1 2 3 4 5 6 12 11 10 09 08 07

TABLE OF CONTENTS

Essential content terms are highlighted and are defined at the bottom of the page where they first appear.

Chapter 1

ICE FISHING

Learn about the history of ice fishing, popular places to ice fish, and fish species.

Fishing enthusiasts don't have to take the winter off from fishing. They can fish on frozen rivers, lakes, and ponds through holes in the ice.

History of Ice Fishing

People have fished through the ice for thousands of years. Many early ice fishers caught fish to survive. They needed the fish for food during the long northern winters.

More than 3,000 years ago, people living in Alaska and Canada made ice fishing spears. They made the spears from wood or animal bone. They cut holes in shallow areas of frozen water. The ice fishers then used the spears to pierce fish that swam underneath the holes.

Avid anglers don't let a little ice get in the way of baiting a hook and catching some fish.

Early ice fishers also used hooks and line. They made the hooks from animal bone or rock. They attached a hook to a horsehair or silk line. They then attached bait to the hook and lowered the line into the water. The ice fishers waited for a fish to bite the bait and become caught on the hook. They then pulled up the line to bring the fish out of the water.

Modern Ice Fishing

By the 1950s, ice fishing became much more popular as a recreational activity in North America. It was no longer necessary for survival. But people still enjoyed ice fishing and eating the fish that they caught.

Modern equipment made ice fishing a bit easier. Power augers allowed ice fishers to cut through the ice quickly. Snowmobiles helped ice fishers travel onto the ice. Ice fishers also began to use modern rods and reels specially made for ice fishing.

Today, people ice fish for a variety of reasons. Many ice fishers enjoy being outdoors. People also ice fish to spend time with family and friends. Some ice fishers simply enjoy the challenge of trying to catch the largest fish they can.

EDGE FACT

Power augers cost at least $300. But they can cut through 18 inches (46 centimeters) of ice in less than a minute.

auger—a tool used for drilling holes in the ice

Ice Fishing Locations

People ice fish on any body of freshwater. Lakes, ponds, streams, and rivers freeze over in winter. The salt water of seas and oceans usually does not freeze.

North Americans mainly ice fish in Canada and the far northern areas of the United States. Even in southern states, water at high elevations can freeze thick enough for ice fishing.

Certain areas are more popular for ice fishing than others. The northeastern United States is a popular ice fishing area. The activity is also common in Minnesota, Wisconsin, and Michigan. Many people ice fish in the eastern Canadian provinces of Quebec and Newfoundland.

EDGE FACT —◌◌

Ice fishing in Arizona? High in the mountains, winters are cold enough for lakes to freeze— even in Arizona.

Italian Style Walleye

Serves: 4 to 6   *Children should have adult supervision.*

Ingredients:

6 walleye fillets
15-ounce (425-gram) can tomato
   sauce
2 teaspoons (10 mL) dried parsley
1 teaspoon (5 mL) Italian seasoning
½ teaspoon (2 mL) dried basil
¼ teaspoon (1 mL) salt
⅛ teaspoon (.5 mL) pepper
4 ounces (113 grams) shredded
   mozzarella cheese

Equipment:

Cooking spray
9- by 13-inch (23- by 33-centimeter)
   cake pan
Medium bowl
Mixing spoon
Metal spatula
Fork

1. Lightly coat cake pan with cooking spray.

2. Place walleye fillets in pan.

3. In bowl, mix the tomato sauce, parsley, Italian seasoning, basil, and salt and pepper together.

4. Pour the mixture over the fillets.

5. Bake uncovered at 350°F (175°C) for 15 minutes.

6. Turn fish over with metal spatula. Sprinkle cheese over the fish.

7. Bake 5 to 10 minutes more. Fish is done when it is hot in the center and it flakes easily when touched with a fork.

Ice fishers sometimes catch northern pike.

Types of Fish

Some people ice fish for panfish. These small fish include bluegill, pumpkinseed, white crappies, and yellow perch. Panfish live in shallow lakes close to shore.

Larger fish species include northern pike, walleye, burbot, and salmon. Lake trout are also popular for ice fishers. Larger fish species often live in lakes. But they also live in streams and rivers.

EDGE FACT

The walleye gets its name from its large staring eyes, which reflect light.

species—a group of fish with similar features

Chapter 2

EQUIPMENT

Learn about rods, bait and lures, and staying warm.

Ice fishers need all the usual fishing gear, such as rods, line, hooks, bait, and lures. But they need some extra equipment too. They need ice augers, tip-ups, warm clothes, a heater, and maybe even an ice house.

Jigging Rods

Ice fishers use jigging rods. These rods are made of either fiberglass or graphite. These materials are lightweight and strong. Most jigging rods are between 2 and 3.5 feet (.6 and 1 meter) long. This length is shorter than regular fishing rods. Ice fishers don't need to cast, so the rods don't need to be long.

Ice fishing rods are shorter than regular fishing rods.

Tip-ups have a flag that pops up when a fish puts pressure on the line.

Jigging rods have a reel to hold fishing line. The reel usually includes a drag system. A reel's drag system allows ice fishers to adjust the pressure on the line as a hooked fish swims. The pressure helps keep the hook in the fish's mouth.

Tip-Ups

Many ice fishers use wooden, metal, or plastic devices called tip-ups. Ice fishers do not need to hold onto a rod when they use tip-ups.

Tip-ups have a frame attached to a reel. The reel has line wound around it. Ice fishers place the frame over the hole. They attach their bait or lure to a hook at the end of the line. They then lower the line into the water.

The reel has a flag with a spring attached to it. The spring causes the flag to pop up when a fish puts pressure on the line. Ice fishers tug the line to set the hook after the flag pops up. This action pushes the hook into the fish's mouth. Ice fishers then bring the fish out of the water.

Tip-ups allow ice fishers to fish in more than one location. But some states set limits on the number of tip-ups fishers may use.

Bait and Lures

Minnows are common live bait. These small fish are usually less than 2 inches (5 centimeters) long. Ice fishers also use worms as bait.

Ice fishers also use dead bait. The scent of dead bait attracts northern pike and salmon.

Lures imitate the color, movement, or scent of food that a fish would eat. One lure is a jigging minnow. It moves sideways when an ice fisher lifts it up and lets it drop. Jigging minnows look like minnows that are trying to escape.

Ice fishers often add live bait to their lures. The combination of a lure and bait can help attract fish.

Bait shops sell all kinds of lures.

Ice fishers also use jigs. These small metal balls are painted to look like an insect's head or a fish's head. Ice fishers use small jigs called teardrops. Teardrops come in a variety of shapes, colors, and styles. Swimming jigs move in a circle when ice fishers lift and drop them. They imitate dying minnows.

Ice fishers need hooks, leaders, and sinkers. Leaders are thin pieces of wire,

jig—a lure that is designed to be jerked up and down

18

6 to 24 inches (15 to 61 centimeters) long. Ice fishers attach them between the lure and the end of the line. They use leaders so that fish with teeth don't cut through their line. Sinkers are small metal objects that keep bait near the water's bottom.

Ice Houses

Many ice fishers use ice houses to help them stay comfortable in cold weather. These shelters can be made from metal, wood, nylon, or plastic.

Portable ice houses are made of nylon or polyethylene. These strong, lightweight materials are resistant to wind and water. Ice fishers can fold up portable ice houses to move them easily. These houses usually fit no more than two people.

Some portable ice houses have a plastic or wooden floor and a metal frame. The floors have holes to fit over the holes in the ice.

EDGE FACT

Some ice fishers make their ice houses as comfortable as their home. They might bring a stereo, TV, or DVD player with them on the ice.

Some ice fishers use permanent ice houses. They use trailers to haul these houses onto the ice. Permanent ice houses are made of metal or wood. Some are big enough to fit more than six people.

Portable heaters warm the inside of the ice houses. Some permanent ice houses have built-in stoves. Outdoor ice fishers might have small heaters to keep their hands and feet warm. The heaters and stoves are powered by gas or propane.

Clothing

Ice fishers need warm clothing. Most ice fishers dress in layers. They can add or remove layers to stay comfortable.

The first clothing layer should keep ice fishers' skin dry. Synthetic fabrics are best for this layer. Some ice fishers choose polyester or polypropylene. Polypropylene is a lightweight material that people use to make plastic products.

Wool makes a good middle layer. Wool keeps people warm even after it gets wet.

Ice fishers stay comfortable in an ice house even on the coldest winter day.

   The final clothing layer is called the shell. The shell should be resistant to wind and water. Gore-Tex is a popular material for this layer. It has a finish that resists moisture. Some ice fishers wear nylon snowmobile suits.

   Ice fishers need other clothing items to stay warm. They need a hat and mittens or gloves. Most ice fishers wear pack boots. These boots have a waterproof rubber sole and a removable wool or felt liner.

EDGE FACT —⌒·◎⟩

Underwater cameras are helpful if you want to know what type of fish is just below your ice house.

Some ice fishers like to use high-tech gadgets. Depth finders, sonar, and even GPS devices help ice fishers make the most of their expedition. But underwater cameras can be even more helpful. They show ice fishers what's going on beneath the ice.

The camera goes in the water as though it were bait. The camera might even be shaped like a fish and be shiny to attract fish. The fisher looks at a screen to see what the camera sees.

A sonar device might show a clump of weeds. Weeds are great cover for many species of fish. But an underwater camera will show the fisher if it's a clump of live weeds or dead weeds. Fish don't like hanging around brown dead weeds.

These cameras cost a few hundred dollars. But it's cool to get an up close view of a hungry fish striking your bait!

Underwater Camera

Depth finders help ice fishers find out where the fish are hiding.

EDGE FACT ⌁

Cold water makes your body heat drop 25 percent faster than air of the same temperature.

Ice Fishing—Tools

Other Ice Fishing Tools

Before heading out on the ice, ice fishers should also make sure to bring a few additional tools. These items can help make their fishing trip more successful.

- **Augers**—either a manual or power auger to cut a hole in the ice; the auger's blades cut into the ice; power augers have an engine that powers the blades
- **Skimmer**—to clear ice chips floating in holes; skimmers have a handle and a scooper with small holes.
- **Depth Finder**—an electronic device that uses sound waves to find underwater objects; a screen shows the location of fish, the water's bottom, and the ice fisher's bait or lure
- **Ice Pick**—a small tool with a sharp point; people who fall through the ice can use it to pull themselves out of the water
- **Gaff**—a long handle with a hook at one end used for pulling up large fish; a gaff should not be used on fish that will be released
- **Rattle Reel**—allows ice fishers hands-free fishing; it rattles when a fish takes the bait.

Inside an Ice House

Ice Fishing—Equipment

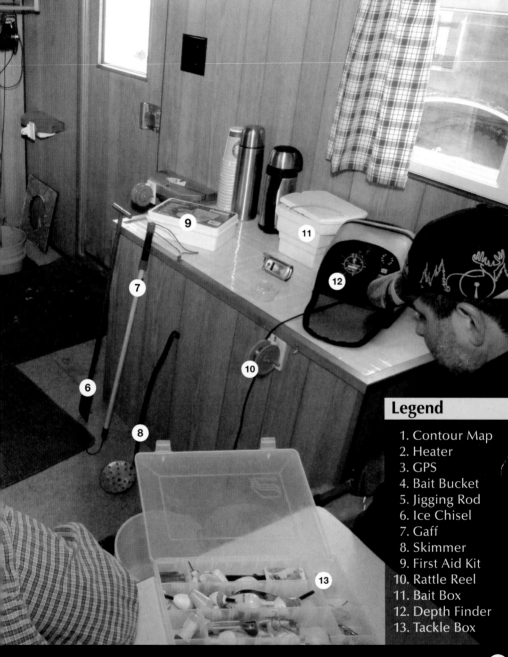

Legend

1. Contour Map
2. Heater
3. GPS
4. Bait Bucket
5. Jigging Rod
6. Ice Chisel
7. Gaff
8. Skimmer
9. First Aid Kit
10. Rattle Reel
11. Bait Box
12. Depth Finder
13. Tackle Box

Chapter 3

SKILLS AND TECHNIQUES

Learn about where and when to fish,
techniques, and bringing in the catch.

Ice fishing requires knowledge and skill. Ice fishers learn about the features and habits of different fish species. They need to decide where to cut holes. They also need to know what to do after a fish strikes.

When to Fish

To catch more fish, ice fishers should learn the common feeding times of different fish species. Walleye feed just before sunrise and just after dark. Bluegill feed in late afternoon.

Ice fishers also use spawning times to decide when to fish. Fish lay eggs during these times. Some species feed more often just before and after they spawn. Most fish spawn in spring. Ice fishers try to catch spawning fish just before the ice begins to thaw.

spawning time—when fish lay eggs

Ice fishers pull upward on the rod quickly when they feel a fish bite.

Locations

Ice fishers look for fish in different areas, depending on what they're fishing for. Panfish live in shallow water. Northern pike and crappies hide in weeds or under logs. Walleye live in deep water.

Ice fishers can use contour maps to choose a fishing location. These maps show the formation of the bottom of a lake. Lines called contours show the water's depth.

In deep lakes, ice fishers might use a bottom finder. These sinkers attach to the hook and line on a tip-up. Ice fishers drop the bottom finder to the water's bottom. They then lift the sinker out of the water and measure the line to find out the water's depth.

contour map—a map with curving lines that show the shape of the bottom of a lake

Ice Fishing—Where to Fish

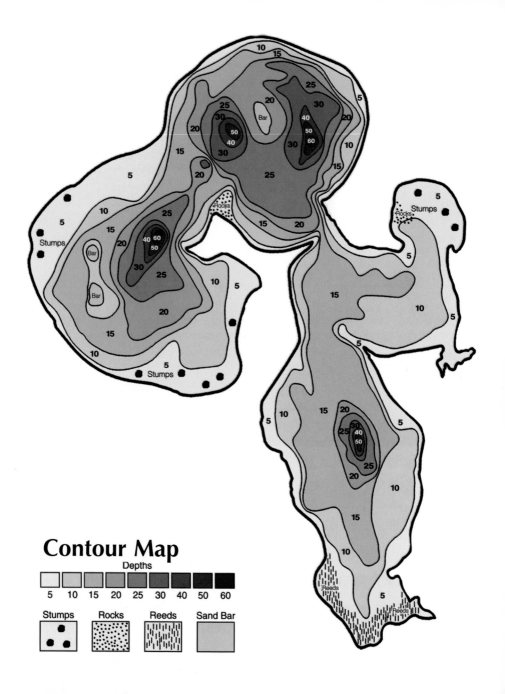

Contour Map

Depths
5 10 15 20 25 30 40 50 60

Stumps Rocks Reeds Sand Bar

Ice fishers carefully remove the hook before either releasing or keeping the fish.

Jigging

Ice fishers use a method called jigging to attract fish. They place the bait or lure about 18 inches (46 centimeters) from the lake bottom. They then gently move the rod upward and let the bait or lure settle. Ice fishers repeat the movement several times to attract fish.

jigging—moving the bait to attract fish

Ice fishers use different jigging techniques depending on the time of day or on the species of fish. Ice fishers might lift their rod quickly upward. This action attracts fish during times they are less likely to feed. A gentle wiggle of the bait or lure attracts panfish.

Landing a Fish

Ice fishers must bring the fish out of the water after it takes the bait or lure. This practice is called landing the fish.

A quick snap of the wrist sets the hook. Ice fishers might let a large fish swim for a while. Once the fish is tired, they reel in the fish to bring the fish out of the water. For fish they want to keep, ice fishers usually keep the fish in a bucket.

EDGE FACT

The world record ice fishing walleye was caught by Father Mariusz Zajac in Canada on January 4, 2005. The fish weighed 18.3 pounds (8.3 kilograms).

Chapter 4

CONSERVATION

Learn about limits, catch-and-release, and protecting fish habitats.

Responsible ice fishers take care of the environment. They follow regulations to protect fish populations and habitats.

Licenses and Regulations

State and provincial government agencies set ice fishing regulations. Regulations require that ice fishers buy fishing licenses when they reach a certain age. This age can vary from 12 to 16.

Government agencies also set limits. Limits regulate the number of fish a person can catch and take home in one day. Limits vary according to the species and time of year.

Some ice fishing regulations limit the number of tip-ups and jigging rods people can use. For example, ice fishers may only be allowed to use a certain number of tip-ups at a time.

Ice fishers must have a current fishing license.

Government agencies also set minimum sizes. Fish smaller than the minimum size must be released. This law helps make sure that fish grow old enough to spawn.

Releasing Fish

Some ice fishers choose to practice catch-and-release fishing. By releasing some fish, they can help make sure there are more big fish available for everyone.

Fish need to be handled gently to prevent injuries to the fish. Ice fishers should put fish back in the water soon after landing them. They should try to keep a fish in the water as they release it. A fish placed in a net can end up with damaged scales.

Fish should not be thrown back into the water. This can stress the fish and lower its chances for survival. Fish should be slid gently back into the water.

Protecting Water Sources

Some water sources are becoming polluted. Waste from factories and chemicals used in farming can pollute water sources. Pollutants can enter the bodies of fish. Fish with

Ice Fishing—Protecting Water Sources

Catch-and-release fishing ensures a healthy fish population.

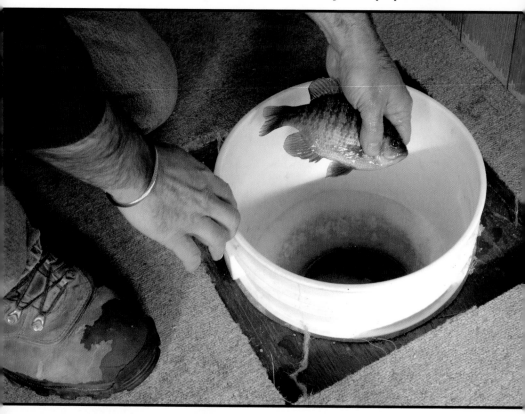

pollutants in them can become sick or die. It might also be unsafe to eat fish that have pollutants in their bodies.

Ice fishers should try to prevent pollution and damage to water sources. They should leave their fishing area as they found it. Responsible fishers place trash in a trash can or take it home with them.

Chapter 5

SAFETY

Learn about walking on ice, signs of unsafe ice, and cold weather cautions.

Ice fishers must be careful on the ice. No ice is completely safe. Ice of any thickness can have weak spots. Ice fishers should look for signs that ice is unsafe. Crunchy ice or ice with a soft top layer is probably weak. Weak ice might also be gray-black instead of clear.

Ice Thickness

The safety of a frozen water area depends on how much weight it needs to support. People can walk on ice that is at least 5 inches (13 centimeters) thick. Ice that is 8 to 12 inches (20 to 30 centimeters) thick can support a car or pick-up.

People sometimes place signs where the ice is weak. These signs help warn others of dangerous conditions. Ice on rivers and streams is about 15 percent weaker than ice on other water areas. The currents prevent thick ice from forming.

With a cold enough winter, the ice can support a heavy truck.

Hypothermia and Frostbite

Ice fishers need to dress for cold weather. Extreme cold weather can cause hypothermia. This condition occurs when a person's body temperature becomes too low. Signs of hypothermia include shivering, slurred speech, and confusion. Hypothermia can cause death.

Long exposure to the cold can cause frostbite. Ice fishers should keep all skin covered in extremely cold weather. Frostbitten skin can be permanently damaged.

Ice House Safety

Gas and propane heaters give off a poisonous gas called carbon monoxide. This gas is colorless and odorless. People inside an ice house who breathe too much of the gas can get carbon monoxide poisoning. This condition causes headaches, sleepiness, and confusion. It can cause death. Ice houses should have at least two openings for the gas to escape.

Responsible ice fishers enjoy their activity while staying safe. They prevent dangerous situations. They share their knowledge with others to help keep the activity safe.

EDGE FACT ⟿

When the temperature is minus 20 degrees Fahrenheit (minus 29 degrees Celsius), frostbite can occur in exposed skin in as little as 30 minutes.

Walleye

Description: Walleye vary in color. They might be various shades of yellow, yellow-red, or yellow-blue. Walleye have small spots above their white underside. They have large eyes. Walleye usually weigh about 3 to 10 pounds (1.4 to 4.5 kilograms).

Habitat: open areas in large lakes; cold, deep water near drop-offs and weeds in lakes

Food: minnows, small fish

Bait and lures: nightcrawlers, minnows, deep diving spoons

Northern Pike

Description: Northern pike are dark bronze. They are long and slim. Their tail and fins are red. Northern pike have rows of white and yellow spots along their sides. Scales cover their cheeks and the upper half of their gill covers. Northern pike have sharp teeth. They usually weigh from 4 to 10 pounds (1.8 to 4.5 kilograms). But many pike weigh much more than that.

Habitat: shallow, weedy areas; near structures

Food: other fish, frogs, ducklings

Bait and lures: large minnows, dead bait, bladebaits, spoons, jigs

Crappies

Description: Crappies are silver-green with black spots. Crappies have one dorsal fin. Black crappies have gill covers with sharp spines. Crappies usually weigh about 1 pound (.5 kilogram).

Habitat: weedy and rocky areas

Food: small fish, insects, worms

Bait and lures: minnows, beetlespins

Perch

Description: Perch can be various shades of green, yellow, or gray. They have dark vertical bars on their sides. Their lower fins are orange-yellow. They usually weigh about 2 pounds (.9 kilogram).

Habitat: open areas in lakes; weedy areas

Food: minnows, insects, worms

Bait and lures: minnows, worms, jigs

GLOSSARY

auger (AW-gur)—a tool that uses a screw mechanism to drill holes

frostbite (FRAWST-bite)—a condition that occurs when cold temperatures freeze skin

habitat (HAB-uh-tat)—the natural place and conditions in which animals live

hypothermia (hye-puh-THUR-mee-uh)—a sometimes deadly condition that can occur when a person's body temperature drops too low

jig (JIG)—a lure that is jerked up and down while fishing; jigs usually look like insects.

pollutant (puh-LOOT-uhnt)—a harmful material that can damage the environment

species (SPEE-sheez)—a group of animals with similar features

synthetic (sin-THET-ik)—something that is made by people rather than found in nature

READ MORE

Klobuchar, Lisa. *Fishing.* Get Going! Hobbies. Chicago: Heinemann, 2006.

Nordin, Hans. *Ice Fishing: Complete Guide to Fishing.* Broomall, Penn.: Mason Crest, 2004.

Seeberg, Tim. *Freshwater Fishing.* Kids' Guides to the Outdoors. Chanhassen, Minn.: Child's World, 2004.

INTERNET SITES

FactHound offers a safe, fun way to find Internet sites related to this book. All of the sites on FactHound have been researched by our staff.

Here's how:

1. Visit *www.facthound.com*

2. Choose your grade level.

3. Type in this book ID **1429608226** for age-appropriate sites. You may also browse subjects by clicking on letters, or by clicking pictures and words.

4. Click on the **Fetch It** button.

FactHound will fetch the best sites for you!

INDEX

The Great Outdoors—Ice Fishing